Life in a Kelp Forest

Text by Mary Jo Rhodes and David Hall
Photographs by David Hall

Undersea Encounters

Children's Press®
A Division of Scholastic Inc.
New York Toronto London Auckland Sydney
Mexico City New Delhi Hong Kong
Danbury, Connecticut

Library of Congress Cataloging-in-Publication Data

Rhodes, Mary Jo, 1957-
  Life in a kelp forest / Mary Jo Rhodes and David Hall; photographs by David Hall.
      p. cm. (Undersea encounters)
  Includes bibliographical references and index.
  ISBN 0-516-24396-9 (lib. bdg.)   0-516-25491-X (pbk.)
  1. Kelp bed ecology—Juvenile literature. 2. Kelps—Juvenile literature. I. Hall, David,
1943 Oct. 2– II. Title. III. Series.
  QH541.5.K4R49 2005
  577.7'8—dc22

                                        2005003686

To Al Spilde and the crews of Sea Venturer *and* Mamro *who showed me the underwater world*
of British Columbia, and to the memory of Jon Hardy, who first introduced me to the wonders
of a California kelp forest.
—D.H.
To my sister Robin, my nephews Andy and Peter, and our unforgettable Zodiac trip to see
the orcas in British Columbia.
—M.J.R.

All photographs in this book were made in British Columbia (Canada) or California,
except for the following: Maine, pages 28, 43 (top right); New Zealand, pages 6, 15, 31;
Tasmania (Australia), pages 7 (inset), 17, 36.

All photographs © 2005 by David Hall.

Sea pens are animals that look like feathers. pg. **22**

Sun stars may look nice, but they are fierce predators! pg. **34**

Life in a Kelp Forest

One "ghost" in the forest has a see-through body. pg. **18**

A bright orange Garibaldi
swims through a giant kelp
forest in California.

chapter 1

Forests in the Sea

If you've ever walked through a forest, you know that many plants and animals live there. But did you know that there are also forests in the ocean? Undersea plants called **kelp** can grow as tall as many trees on land. Like a forest on land, kelp forests shelter many kinds of animals and plants. These undersea forests are found near the seashore in cool or cold ocean water.

Ocean Plants

Most large ocean plants are called **seaweeds** (SEE-weeds). "Kelp" is the name used for a group of large yellow or brown seaweeds. Under some conditions, kelp plants can also appear green. Other kinds of seaweeds are usually red or green.

Kelp grows very fast in cold water. Cold water is rich in **nutrients** (NU-tree-ents) that help plants grow. Kelp grows so fast that an entire undersea forest can appear in a single summer.

6

floats

stipes

blades

A Tree in the Ocean

Kelp plants cling tightly to the rocky seafloor with a **holdfast** (top inset). The stems of kelp plants are called **stipes**. The leaves are called **blades**. Many stipes and blades twisted around one another form **fronds**.

The thin, rubbery stipes cannot support a very tall plant. Instead, the plants have floats that are filled with air. They are like small balloons. These floats allow the kelp to grow very tall.

Giant kelp plants can grow as tall as a tree in just a few months.

Giant Kelp

The tallest of all ocean plants is called giant kelp. It may grow up to 120 feet (37 meters). That's taller than most trees! Lots of giant kelp plants together form undersea forests. These forests are found along the Pacific Coast of North America, especially in California. Giant kelp forests are also found in southern Australia, New Zealand, and South America.

Fronds of giant kelp often grow tall enough to reach the surface of the water. Even so, they continue to grow. Fronds from many kelp plants may float on the surface. As they grow longer, they form a thick mat called a canopy. Seabirds, seals, and sea otters hunt and rest in the canopy of kelp forests.

Giant kelp fronds floating on the surface of the water form a kelp canopy.

Forest Fact

Giant kelp is one of the fastest-growing plants on Earth. It can grow as much as the length of your arm in a single day!

Black rockfish find
shelter among
smaller kelp plants.

Bull Kelp

As you travel north of California along the Pacific Coast, the undersea forest changes. These northern forests are formed mostly of bull kelp. Smaller kelps and seaweeds are also common. Bull kelp grows almost as tall as giant kelp, but is much stronger. It can survive the powerful ocean waves and currents in colder parts of the world.

Bull kelp has a single, long stipe with blades growing out from the top.

Bull kelp looks different from giant kelp. Each plant has just one thick stipe with a single, large float at the end. Long blades trail out from the float and form a canopy on the surface.

Hermit crabs nibble at the stipe of a kelp plant that has fallen to the sea floor.

chapter 2

Living With Kelp

Like plants on land, kelp plants need sunlight to grow. A kelp plant takes in the sunlight and turns it into stored energy. In turn, animals eat the plants. **Predators** (PRED-uh-tors) eat those other animals. This passing of energy from one living thing to the next is called a food chain.

Kelp forests not only provide food for animals, they also create homes for them. Many smaller creatures grow on the kelp. Others hide among the blades and holdfasts. Predators also lurk among the kelp plants in search of **prey** (PRAY).

Topsnails eat kelp, and also some of the small animals that live on kelp.

Kelp as Food

Many animals, such as snails and crabs, live on the kelp plants. Colorful topsnails eat both kelp and the tiny animals that grow on it. Kelp crabs eat kelp too, but some also wear it! Young crabs sometimes tear off a piece of kelp and attach it to themselves to serve as a disguise. Even the dying kelp plants that fall to the forest floor are eaten by hermit crabs, snails, and sea urchins.

Sea urchins, shown below, also eat kelp. They sometimes eat the kelp holdfasts, so that the plants float away.

Kelp as Home

Kelp plants do not have flowers, although it may look that way. What appear to be flowers are really animals called **sea anemones** (uh-NEM-o-nees). Each anemone has many long tentacles (TEN-tuh-culs) lined with dozens of stingers. Tiny floating animals called plankton are caught and killed by the stingers. Small sea anemone relatives that live on kelp are called hydroids.

Colonies of moss animals also live on kelp plants. They look like patches of white moss growing on kelp blades. These animals strain sea-water through a fine net to trap plankton. This method of catching food is called **filter feeding**.

Fish live among the kelp plants, too. The kelp clingfish has a "suction cup" on its belly for holding on to the kelp. Schools of black rockfish swim among the kelp plants. They can hide from predators there.

The "flowers" growing on kelp plants are actually animals called sea anemones.

The small white patches on kelp are colonies of moss animals, or bryozoans.

Forest Ghosts

One forest creature has a body that you can see through. This ghost-like animal is a hooded nudibranch. It has a "net" that opens and closes to trap plankton. By the end of summer, kelp may be covered with hundreds of these animals.

Hunting on Kelp

Predators also live on kelp. **Nudibranchs** (NU-duh-branks) are related to snails, but have no shell. They eat the hydroids, moss animals, and sponges that grow on kelp. Some nudibranchs are brightly colored to warn other animals that they taste bad.

The kelpfish is the same size and shape as a kelp blade. It can even change color to match the kelp. The kelpfish hides among the plants, waiting to pounce on small fish or shrimps.

A kelpfish waits to pounce on smaller fish.

Two nudibranchs are munching on
sea squirts, soft-bodied animals
attached to rocks on the forest floor.

chapter 3

The Kelp Forest Floor

The floor of the forest is a busy place. Many more animals live there than on the kelp itself. Most are **invertebrates** (in-VER-tuh-brates). This means they do not have a backbone.

Different animals move through the forest in different ways. Some attach themselves to rocks and barely move. Others crawl or glide slowly from place to place. The forest is filled with animals moving at their own pace.

Orange sea pens live in the sand patches between the rocks.

Stuck on a Rock

Some stinging animals attach themselves to rocks on the forest floor. These include sea anemones and several kinds of coral. Corals are similar to anemones, except they usually grow in groups or "colonies." Orange sea pens are closely related to corals. They anchor themselves in the sand between the rocks. All of these stinging animals travel very little, if at all.

Gliding on One Foot

Some animals with a shell have a kind of "foot." Snails, chitons (KI-tons), and their relatives are **mollusks** (MOL-lusks). These animals glide along slowly on their foot. Sea slugs like nudi-branchs have no shell and can glide a bit faster.

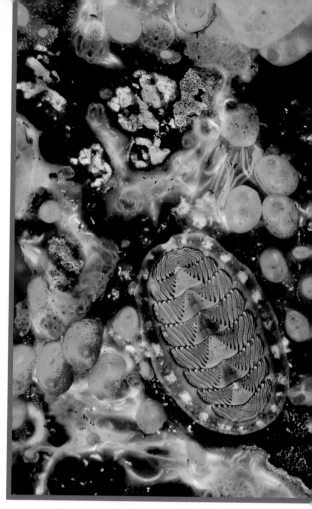

A lined chiton is surrounded by orange sea squirts.

Other mollusks have two shells. These animals use their foot in different ways. A clam uses its foot to anchor itself in sand. A mussel uses its foot to attach itself to a rock. Many scallops are not attached to anything at all. They can swim short distances by opening and closing their two shells very rapidly.

Mollusks also feed in different ways. Chitons and most snails eat plants. Clams, mussels, oysters, and scallops are filter feeders. Nudibranchs are predators that eat other animals.

Crawling on Many Feet

Sea stars and sea urchins might beat a snail in a race, but not by much! These creatures crawl slowly through the forest, moving with hundreds of tiny tube feet. A sea star's tube feet line the underside of its arms. A sea urchin's tube feet are located on the surface of its body, among its spines.

Sea stars are predators. They prey on many different invertebrate animals. Sea cucumbers are fat, wormlike animals with tentacles at one end. Many of them are filter feeders, while others are scavengers. A scavenger feeds on dead and decaying plants or animals.

A leather sea star feeds
on white sea anemones.
Nearby is a red sea urchin.

Fins As Feet

Some kinds of fish also live on the forest floor. Most of them are predators in disguise. These fishes wait to pounce on smaller animals. Occasionally they swim in search of a new hunting spot. A few, like the small grunt sculpin, shown here, do not swim. Instead, they "walk" slowly on their fins.

Running on Legs

Some of the swiftest animals on the forest floor run on several pairs of legs. Their legs bend at joints, just as our legs bend at the knee. Most of these animals are **crustaceans** (crus-TAY-shuns). Crustaceans include crabs, lobsters, and shrimps. Some crustaceans eat plants, and others are predators. Many crabs are scavengers.

A candy-striped shrimp hides among the tentacles of a sea anemone.

This crab lives inside an old barnacle shell.

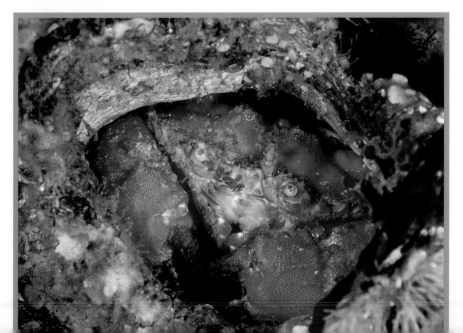

27

The northern lobster is a giant of the Atlantic coast. It has two powerful claws. One is for crushing shells, the other is for cutting and tearing.

chapter 4

Giants of the Kelp Forest

Kelp plants are not the only things that grow extra large in cold water. Nutrients in the water affect the entire food chain. Some of the animals found in northern Pacific kelp forests are the largest of their kind in the world.

A Giant Anemone

The giant plumose anemone is the tallest of all sea anemones. With its body fully extended, it can be as tall as a

The 3-foot (1-m) plumose sea anemone is the tallest in the world.

kitchen countertop. This giant has more than one hundred tentacles. The same anemone is also found along the northern Atlantic Coast.

Jellyfish Giant

The largest jellyfish in the world sometimes visits the kelp forest. It is called the lion's mane jellyfish. Part of its body hangs down like the long, yellow hair of a male lion. The tentacles of this giant can be as long as a school bus!

A jellyfish is like an upside-down, swimming sea anemone. Its tentacles are lined with stingers. The tentacles hang down from a round body part called the bell. Jellyfish swim by opening and closing the bell like an umbrella.

A lion's mane jellyfish swims near the surface of the water. Its body can be up to 6 feet (2 m) across.

Giant Pacific Octopus

The largest octopus in the world lives along the Pacific Coast. It is called the giant Pacific octopus. This giant lives in rocky dens on the forest floor. Like most octopuses, the giant octopus is skilled in the art of disguise. It has the ability to change its shape and color to match almost any background.

Weighing up to 100 pounds (45 kilograms) or more, the giant Pacific octopus is the largest in the world.

The wolf-eel is a shy giant. It spends most of its time hiding in a rocky den.

Wolf-Eel

The wolf-eel is the world's largest blenny. Blennies are slender fish that are usually just a few inches long. But the wolf-eel is a giant. It grows to almost 8 feet (2.5 m) in length. It has strong teeth and powerful jaws for breaking open the shells of its prey. Wolf-eels may look scary, but they are harmless to people.

Giant Sun Stars

Most sea stars, or starfish, have five arms. Large sea stars with more than five arms are called sun stars. The giant sunflower star is the largest sea star in the world. It can be 4 feet (1.2 m) across and have twenty-four arms. This large sea star is the ultimate forest floor predator. It will eat almost anything it can catch, including scallops, sea urchins, and crabs.

Other large sun stars are also found in northern Pacific kelp forests. They are smaller than the sunflower star. Still, they are fierce predators. The sun stars shown at right (top to bottom) are the rose sun star, orange sun star, and striped sun star.

A swell shark swims through a giant kelp forest. When threatened, it may swallow water to swell its body and appear larger.

chapter 5

Kelp Forest Fish

Many fish find food and shelter in undersea forests. Some swim through the forest in groups, or "schools." Some live on or among the kelp plants. Many kinds of fish live on the forest floor, hidden among the rocks and kelp holdfasts.

Unlike snails, crabs, or sea stars, fish are **vertebrates** (VER-tuh-brates). Like people, they have an inner skeleton and a backbone. Fish also have fins for swimming and gills for breathing underwater.

On the Forest Floor

Greenlings are among the more common fish that live on the forest floor. They have long, narrow bodies. The male and female kelp greenling are colored so differently from one another that they were once thought to be different species. The lingcod is a giant greenling that can be more than 4 feet (1.5 m) long. It hides among the kelp plants, waiting to attack smaller prey.

Rockfish are found in Pacific Coast kelp forests. Most kinds of adult rockfish swim in schools among the kelp plants. The China rockfish lives on the forest floor. Rockfish are beautiful to look at, but don't try to touch one! You might receive a painful sting from the poisonous spines in its fins.

Forest Fact

Rockfish spend the early part of their lives in the kelp forest canopy. Hidden among the kelp blades and fronds, the young fish are safe from predators.

The kelp greenling (above) and the China rockfish (below) are two common members of the forest floor community. Both are predators that feed on a variety of smaller fish and invertebrates.

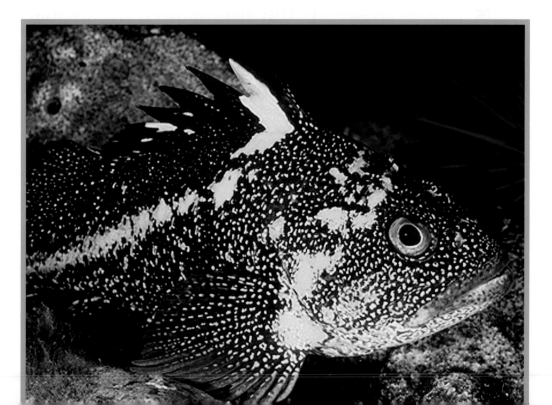

An Irish lord sculpin rests among white sea anemones.

Lord of the Forest

Like rockfish, sculpins are commonly found in Pacific Coast undersea forests. Most kinds of sculpins live on the sea floor. Many of them are able to change color to blend in with their surroundings.

Most sculpins are predators that ambush their prey. The Irish lord sculpin will attack and eat almost anything smaller than itself, including fish and crabs, or even a small octopus.

An Underwater Wilderness

A kelp forest is a magical place filled with giant plants and unusual animals. Many kelp forests have never been explored. In fact, most people

An Irish lord sculpin hides among pink soft corals and white sea anemones. The sculpin is lying in wait, ready to attack a small fish that comes too close.

This diver is in a giant kelp forest off the coast of California.

are not even aware that this underwater wilderness exists.

Like any forest, a kelp forest can be harmed by human activities. For example, overfishing and pollution can be serious problems. Global warming is also a threat. Kelp plants can only survive in cold water.

If we treat this underwater wilderness with respect, it will remain healthy. The kelp forest is still waiting to be explored. Perhaps someday you'll be the one to do it!

More Kelp Forest Animals

Northern Basketstar
This filter-feeding relative of sea stars has branching arms.

Gooseneck Barnacles
These filter-feeding crustaceans are related to crabs and shrimps.

Sea Cucumber
This sea star relative has a fat body and branching tentacles.

Scallop
Scallops can swim by opening and closing their shells rapidly.

Yellow Sponge
Sponges are simple animals with no brains, nerves, or muscles.

Pink Hydroids
Hydroids are tiny, stinging relatives of sea anemones.

Glossary

blade the part of a kelp plant that looks like a leaf. *(pg. 7)*

crustacean (crus-TAY-shun) an animal with several pairs of jointed legs and an outer skeleton or shell. Crabs, shrimps, and lobsters are crustaceans. *(pg. 27)*

filter feeding a method of feeding that involves straining seawater with a fine net. Tiny, floating animals and plants are trapped and then eaten. *(pg. 16)*

fronds the stipes and blades of giant kelp plants twisted together. *(pg. 7)*

holdfast the part of a kelp plant that attaches it to the seafloor. *(pg. 7)*

invertebrate (in-VER-tuh-brate) an animal with no backbone. Snails, crabs, insects, worms, sea stars, and sea anemones are invertebrates. *(pg. 21)*

kelp large seaweeds that are usually brown or yellow. *(pg. 5)*

mollusk (MOL-lusk) a soft-bodied invertebrate animal, usually with a hard shell. Snails, clams, and scallops are mollusks. *(pg. 23)*

nudibranch (NU-duh-brank) a mollusk related to a snail but with no hard shell. *(pg. 19)*

nutrient (NU-tree-ent) a substance that plants and animals need to live or grow. *(pg. 6)*

predator (PRED-uh-tor) an animal that hunts and kills other animals for food. *(pg. 13)*

prey (PRAY) an animal that is hunted and killed for food. *(pg. 14)*

sea anemone (uh-NEM-o-nee) an invertebrate animal with stinging tentacles. *(pg. 16)*

seaweed (SEE-weed) a simple ocean plant that produces no flowers or seeds and needs sunlight to grow. Seaweed is a kind of algae. *(pg. 6)*

stipe the "stem" of a kelp plant. *(pg. 7)*

vertebrates (VER-tuh-brates) animals with a backbone. Fishes, frogs, snakes, turtles, birds, and mammals are all vertebrates. *(pg. 37)*

Learn More About Kelp Forests

Books

Cole, Melissa and Brandon Cole. *Kelp Forests*. San Diego: Blackbirch Press, 2004.

Hall, Howard. *The Kelp Forest: The Ebb and Flow of Life in the Sea's Richest Habitat*. Englewood Cliffs, NJ: Silver Burdett Press, 1995.

Swanson, Diane and Dale Sanders. *The Emerald Sea: Exploring the Underwater Wilderness of the Pacific Northwest and Alaska*. Vancouver, B.C.: Alaska Northwest Books, 1993.

Wu, Norbert. *Beneath the Waves: Exploring the Hidden World of the Kelp Forest*. San Francisco: Chronicle Books, 1992.

Web sites

Kelp Forest Exhibit
Monterey Bay Aquarium, Monterey, California
(www.mbayaq.org/efc/efc_hp/hp_kelp_exhibit.asp)

Kelp Forests
(http://life.bio.sunysb.edu/marinebio/kelpforest.html)

Inch in a Pinch: Kelp Forests
(www.inchinapinch.com/hab_pgs/marine/kelp/kelp.htm)

Index

About the Authors

After earning degrees in zoology and medicine, **David Hall** has worked for the past twenty-five years as both a wildlife photojournalist and a physician. David's articles and photographs have appeared in hundreds of calendars, books, and magazines, including *National Geographic, Smithsonian, Natural History,* and *Ranger Rick*. His underwater images have won many major awards including *Nature's Best,* BBC Wildlife Photographer of the Year, and Festival Mondial de l'Image Sous-Marine.

Mary Jo Rhodes received her M.S. in Library Service from Columbia University and was a librarian for the Brooklyn Public Library. She later worked for ten years in children's book publishing in New York City. Mary Jo lives with her husband, John Rounds, and two teenage sons, Jeremy and Tim, in Hoboken, New Jersey.

About the Consultant

Karen Gowlett-Holmes, one of Australia's leading marine biologists, is a recognized expert on the classification of mollusks and other marine invertebrates. She has worked as Collection Manager of Marine Invertebrates for the South Australia Museum and for Australia's scientific and industrial research organization, CSIRO. Karen has written a number of popular articles and book chapters, and has published more than forty scientific papers.